Inking To The Infinity

Dipping into infinity pool of emotions

Anamika Bajpai

BookLeaf Publishing

India | USA | UK

Made with ❤ on the BookLeaf Publishing Platform
www.bookleafpub.in
www.bookleafpub.com

Dedication

Well, all these years we have heard, There is always a
woman behind a successful man.
But, I am highly grateful to the men of my family as I
get huge motivation & due support whenever needed.
I dedicate this book to my near & dear Ones,
My Dear Papa, My Inspiration Mr V.K.Bajpai
My Dear Husband, My Love Mr. Akhil K. Pandey
My Dear partner in good & bad deeds, my sweet bro Mr.
Ankit K. Bajpai

Last but not least, My Rock Solid, My Dearest Mummy
'Mrs. Savitri Bajpai'.
My Dear Loving Friends Shweta, Chanda, Nishu & Ashu.

Preface

This evocative collection of 21 poems delves into the complexities of human emotions and behaviors, crafting a poetic narrative that is both deeply personal and universally relatable. With themes of love, affection, and warmth woven throughout, this book is a moving celebration of the human spirit.

There is one Poem - In a Way, which has hidden meaningful message, that's already been dedicated to its special owner. Stay curious until you read it all. Happy reading.

Acknowledgements

I am deeply grateful for the opportunity to have worked on this book, which has been a catalyst for personal growth and transformation. When faced with self-doubt and uncertainty, I found the courage to persevere and push forward. This journey would not have been possible without the unwavering support and encouragement of my loved ones. I would like to express my sincere appreciation to my Father, Mother, Husband, and Brother, who have been my guiding light and source of inspiration throughout this journey. And importantly thanking book leaf publication who is responsible for publishing my work.Thank you.

1. In a way

I never thought enough of you.
Like Sun & moon or my heart.
Out of all its you whose
Virtues holds with gentle & warm touch,
Even you embrace the voice inside me, as its
Yours unique quality,
Out of that I feel again myself.
Untill I set anything certain in my life.
A beautiful story & connection found "us".
Kicks in the reality.
Hours of messages & emotions
In a day, Rather loud but meaningful
Lots of joy delivers in a way.

2. Wander Alone

Wander Alone
I wished to wander alone in nights,
With Full moon & star-like bright.
many awaken many asleep
some are engrossed in deep
Oh but others in cheat.
Long Road No one but Marie with my side.
My bestie My pride.
shining whenever wind blows high.
Sending pain of broken leaves.
Ne'er give up on those streets
Where once Friends met, eyes got wet,
Dreams left, insane threat
even years passed away,
but Cheering together again like
it was yesterday.

3. I like you in my poetry

I still like you in my poetry
I still hide you in my poetry
I may die with you in my poetry
There are rebels in me
but they found shelter in you
even when I am shy in my poetry
And you wished to create this story
The license to most dangerous road
which became A beautiful mystery
Amidst cold nights which derive some beauty
how it turned out like a treaty
The nearer I go, the prettier you seem
but what scared me most
a painful history
Rather repeat, I will form one diary
And then
I 'll hide you in my diary!!

4. Fierce Like A Fire Ball

Flying so higher ,so higher she's dying .
Failing so harder ..so harder she's trying
Breathing so deeper , so deeper she's relying..
Oh this bloody message passing on
Your not only who's watching over.
Mean the people, joking around.
tactics on, bullying on
Fiercely she, Just bang on!!
Jumping into Cold water, like a fire ball
harming none but head on
Slaying still, she is master of all.
Replying still, she's still replying!!

5. Go Green

Though Red is so far seen
But why my eyes favourite is Green
several hearts be blood red But you know
Blood runs on the Green.
Wonder how the Blood is biased
for living ones it's red & For others its Green.
When red Ages then it's old & materialistic
But when Green does so we have more to eat.
Red in veins is still so mean
Day & Night chopping But Green
the giver is happy in being.
Lets Go Green without being Mean.

6. Do not stop Believing me

While shiver resides on your hand,
Feel like outta my mind
Cant see world exist for me
Just like topsy turvy land

When you call the God
Wanna have courage to have that sword
could kill all your odd

O my dear, O dear Chief,
Just hold my hands & have faith in God.
All your efforts must be crowned, if not
I must be dumb & must be drowned

Your fatty Aging Skin,
Cant disparage me.
I am none but yours Akin.
Do not stop Believing me.

7. The Captain Of the House

The family's Proud
Who is one in the Crowd,
The selfless soul.
The captain of the house.

With every step, with every fall,
She's there to catch, to hear the call.
Through laughter and tears, through every test,
She stands strong, and does her best.

Her love is pure, her heart is kind,
A shelter from life's turbulent wind.
The family's rock, the guiding star,
A mother's love, near and far."

8. Fight is my might

Did you Hide the truth again
was it a tough part of the day
To make happy Tomorrow Again
make sure you don't see mirror today.
The fight itself is the real prize
Not the trophy, nor the victor's cries
For in the struggle, I find my might
Not the trophy, nor the victor's cries
For in the struggle, I find my might
A resilience that shines, like a beacon in flight.

9. Us

The Love chose affection,
You have choosen me.
Moments have that Magic,
To make two of "Us" As "We".

You wanted to say but you dint,
since you were honest
The Universe made some progress
Truth came out Deepest & Purest.

Thanks for the beautiful confess.

10. This Time It was different

The bag full of Hopes, Flying away from home
Life changes, leaving it all.
The room, once filled with laughter and tears,
Now echoes with memories, through all the years.

Although I did say Goodbyes before,
But this hit different, altogether.
No more a day talk, No more good laugh
The world outside Country, vast & wide,
A canvas waiting, for my story to reside.

I take a good sit on balcony with being sun kissed
felt Happy & sad on the same time,
The journey begins, with a mix of fear and cheer,
As I spread my wings, and let my spirit clear.

I thought we created home of our choice.
But see it shaped me with various color of butterflies.

11. The window Dance

He stands outside, with heart aflame,
Convinced the girl behind the window's his claim to
fame.
He thinks she dances, just for his eyes,
A secret performance, beneath the twilight skies.

He recalls the day she smiled at him,
A fleeting glance, that sparked a whim.
A memory he's treasured, and often replayed,
A moment's connection, that his heart has swayed.

The window's a screen, a canvas so bright,
Reflecting images, that dance through the night.
He's captivated by the illusion, so real and so fine,
A puppet on strings, of his own heart's design.

But as he lingers, the TV show ends its play,
And the girl inside closes the curtains, revealing the
truth of the day:
A reflection of a TV program, a trick of the light.

12. A new Girl in Jersey

She left India's spice for Jersey's slice,
Traded masala chai for coffee & ice.
From saris to sneakers, she made the switch,
And learned to pump her fist, with a Jersey twitch.

She marveled at the turnpike's crazy pace,
And laughed at accents, that sounded like a different
place.
She discovered Wawa, and its magical ways,
And learned to order a sub, with Jersey's special sways.

Her Indian friends back home, would often tease,
"Jersey girl, you're losing your curry ease!"
But she'd reply with a grin, "Hey, I'm doing fine,
I've got my Jersey attitude, and my hot chocolate is on
my mind!"

She danced to Taylor Swift, with her desi flair,
And taught her Jersey friends, how to Bollywood air.
She merged two worlds, with laughter and with cheer,

And proved that humor's universal, no matter where
you're from, my dear!

13

13. Better Half

We sit on our porch, hand in hand,
Watching sunsets, in our golden land.
Sixty years of love, of laughter and of tears,
Our hearts still beating, through all the passing years.

You look at me, with eyes so bright,
And I see the sparkle, of our wedding night.
We talk of memories, of children grown,
Of dreams we chased, and stories yet untold.

I recall the way, you used to dance,
With steps so light, and a heart so prance.
You remember my jokes, and my crazy grin,
And how we'd laugh together, until our sides would give
in.

In these golden years, our love shines bright,
A flame that burns, with warmth and delight.
We'll cherish every moment, every laugh, every tear,
Together, forever, my love, my dear.

14. Falling in Love Once or Twice

Is it a fall, a tumble, a stumble into love?
Or is it a choice, a brave step from above?
Do we lose ourselves, or do we find our way?
In the depths of another's eyes, on a given day?

Perhaps it's both, a dance between fate and might,
A surrender to emotions, and a courageous delight.
For to love is to risk, to bare our soul,
To be vulnerable, and to make ourselves whole.

It takes courage to love again, to open up our hearts,
To let go of fears, and to never depart.
From the thrill of the unknown , to the comfort of the
familiar,
Love requires bravery, and a willingness to be together.

So is it a fall, or a choice? Maybe it's both,
A leap of faith, and a journey to the heart's troth.

For love is an adventure, that requires us to be bold,
To fall, to choose, and to never grow old.

16

15. She is so Quiet

She is so quiet that,
Family is peaceful
No matter what is in her heart
but no scratch on family pride.

She is so quiet that
World does not feel guilty.
Family asked to be happy & right
Forgot to ask to raise your voice.

Eventually
Her heart Paradise
Resides in her Children's book's sky.
Where she recalls everything but kept Quiet.

Now is the Time to re live
In the motherhood she has got new life
She is ready to Raise her voice
& Decided to No more Cry.

16. No matter what, She Stays

She waits and watches, as her loved ones depart,
With hearts that are heavy and a soul that's torn apart.
She stands strong and silent, with tears that she hides,
And prays for their safety, with a love that won't subside.

No matter the distance, no matter the test,
She'll hold on to love, and be our soldier's best.
She'll keep the home fires burning, and the family ties
strong,
And be the rock that holds, when our soldier can't be
long.

She'll face the lonely nights, and the endless days,
With courage in her heart, and a love that never fades.
She'll be the wind beneath, our soldier's wings,
And give them the strength, to do their duty and bring.

No matter what comes her way, she'll stand tall and true,

With the love of our soldier, forever shining through.
She'll be the home, the haven, the heart that beats for
two,
And welcome our soldier, back home, with a love that's
strong and true.

17. "Dopehar" of my Village

The city's din and noise, it fade away,
The villagers gathering under banyan and "Neem" tree is
long lasting way.
Where " charcha and baithak " were more in craze.
The village calls,
A place where love and peace, like wildflowers seize.

The thatched roofs and mud walls, they welcome me
home,
The familiar faces, with their warm and gentle tone.
Wonderful neighbourhood only there reside.
The "Chulhe ki makke di roti te Sarson da saag" is food
paradise.

That sant mahant aagman, pravachan, & nukkad ki chai,
The laughter of children, as they dance fully replaced
with future worries now.
The scent of woodsmoke, cows milk ,first rain's smell,
and the taste of fresh air,
A sense of belonging, that's beyond compare.

The city's pace and stress, they slowly unwind,
As I reconnect with nature, and leave my worries behind.
The village's gentle rhythm, it soothes my soul,
A sense of peace and calm, that makes me whole.

18. Their Hope

Their days are filled, with memories of the past,
Their evenings spent, in hopes that will forever last.
They sit on their porch, hand in hand, and wait,
For the sound of footsteps, that will bring joy to their
gate.

Their only child, a soldier brave and true,
Fighting for the country, with a heart that's strong and
new.
They've waited years, through letters and calls,
For the day he'll return, and hear their joyful walls.

Their hearts are filled, with love and pride,
For the man their son has become, with a spirit that
won't subside.
They know he'll come home, when his duty's done,
And they'll welcome him back, with a love that's never
undone.

The wait is long, but their hope remains strong,

For the day their son will return, and sing their favorite
song.
They'll hold him close, and never let go,
Their love for him, forever shining bright, like a beacon
in the snow.

19. Close your eyes

In the silence, I hear your heartbeat
A rhythm that echoes, our love so unique
I take your hand, and pull you close to me
Feeling your warmth, is where I'm meant to be

Close your eyes, and let me take you away
To a place where love, is the only thing that stays
Close your eyes, and let me hold you tight
In this moment, everything feels just right

Your lips, they whisper, sweet nothings in my ear
Your touch, it sets my soul, on fire, year after year
I look into your eyes, and see a love so true
Forever with you, is where I want to be, with you

Close your eyes, and let me hold you tight
In this moment, everything feels just right

We'll dance under the stars, on a night so clear
Our love, it will shine bright, and banish all fear

We'll cherish every moment, and never let go
In your arms, is where I want to stay, forevermore

26

So close your eyes, and let me love you tonight
In the morning light, our love will still shine bright.

20. Its You Vs you

Who am I, and what's my fate?
A wanderer, or a soul that's great?

You are a dreamer, with a heart so bright
A shining star, that lights up the night

What holds me back, from reaching my goal?
Is it fear, or doubt, that takes its toll?

It's the voices in your head, that whisper low
But you have the power, to let them go

How do I find, my inner strength and might?
How do I rise, above the darkness of night?

You find it in your heart, where love resides
You rise above, by letting your spirit glide

What's the purpose, of this life I lead?
Is it to chase happiness, or to plant a seed?

It's to grow and learn, to evolve and thrive
To leave a mark, that touches hearts and lives

Can I forgive, and let go of the past?
Can I love myself, and forever last?

You can and you will, for you are strong and free
You'll rise above, and be the best version of thee"

21. Shiva Shakti : The Infinity

In realms of the gods, where stars are born,
A tale of love and union, forever sworn.
Shiva, the destroyer, with heart of stone,
Mourned the loss of Sati, his love, his own.

His meditation deep, his soul astray,
The universe suffered, in disarray.
The gods, in council, decided to intervene,
To awaken Shiva, and his heart to retrieve.

Kamadeva, the god of love, with arrow bright,
Pierced Shiva's heart, and broke his meditation's night.
As Shiva's eyes opened, he beheld a sight,
Parvati, the mountain princess, shining with delight.

Her beauty and devotion, like a rose in bloom,
Captured Shiva's heart, and filled his soul's room.
He saw in her, the reincarnation of his past,
Sati, his beloved, forever to forever last.

Their love rekindled, like a flame that never fades,
Shiva and Parvati, in each other's gaze, were made.
Their union was cosmic, a balance of masculine and
feminine might,
Ardhanarishvara, the half-male, half-female form, shone
with delight.

With Shiva's destructive power, and Shakti's creative
force,
The universe was reborn, in a cosmic, loving course.
Their love became the harmony, that governs the
universe's sway,
A dance of opposites, in perfect balance, night and day.

In this cosmic waltz, of give and take,
Shiva and Shakti, their love, for eternity, will make.
A symbol of union, of masculine and feminine as one,
Ardhanarishvara, the cosmic couple, forever has just
begun.

Their love story etched, in the cosmos' fabric so fine,
Inspires us mortals, to seek union, heart and soul
entwine.
For in the cosmic dance, of Shiva and Shakti's love,
We find the balance, of opposites, sent from above.

May their love inspire, our own hearts to entwine,
In the cosmic harmony, of masculine and feminine
divine.
For in the union of opposites, we find the cosmic whole,
Shiva and Shakti's love, forever our hearts and souls will
enfold.